Together We Stand

Edited By Donna Samworth

First published in Great Britain in 2020 by:

YoungWriters®
Est. 1991

Young Writers
Remus House
Coltsfoot Drive
Peterborough
PE2 9BF
Telephone: 01733 890066
Website: www.youngwriters.co.uk

All Rights Reserved
Book Design by Ashley Janson
© Copyright Contributors 2020
Softback ISBN 978-1-80015-057-7

Printed and bound in the UK by BookPrintingUK
Website: www.bookprintinguk.com
YBW0450D

Foreword

Expressing emotions, ordering the mind's turmoil or simply celebrating what's around them, poets and authors have used the written word to great effect for centuries. And when the UK, along with many other parts of the world, went into lockdown in March 2020 due to a global pandemic, we once again turned to the art of writing to help us through.

Around the country we were seeing acts of selflessness; acts of unity as people came together to show their appreciation for key workers and the NHS; and acts of sacrifice as people followed the rules of lockdown to slow the spread of Coronavirus.

We created Write to Unite as a way for people to share their optimism and messages of hope, as a way to focus their feelings of anxiety and frustration, or as a way to give thanks to those who made sacrifices for the greater good, working tirelessly to keep the country going.

When we launched Write to Unite we hoped it would give writers something to focus on during lockdown, and the response was beyond anything we had expected. Now we hope that this resulting collection of poems, prose and fiction will offer solace, hope, or even just pure entertainment to you the reader as you explore the experiences and emotions of ordinary people across the country going through something extraordinary.

Write to Unite reminds us that no matter what we face, we can get through it together.

Contents

Independent Entries

Ebony Bushby (11)	1
Lauren Nkosephayo Johnson	2
Umu Hawa Kemokai (10)	7
Yasaa Uddin (10)	8
Lacey-Jai Stokes (10)	11
Anhaar Ishak (11)	12
Rajan Kumar (11)	14
Miar Abouarghoub (12)	16
Himani Juneja (12)	18
Aaminah Moosa (11)	20
Ansh Bahl	22
Suraiya Rahman (12)	25
Alina Ahmed (13)	26
Eesa Raza (7)	28
Savannah Banger (5)	29
Angelo Eleazar Gallaza (12)	30
Patricia Nsue Nvomo (12)	32
Masa Barakat (12)	33
Esha Furrukh (13)	34
Jorja Lacey Morgan (10)	35
Jamil Ladha (12)	36
Saachi Jawa (10)	38
Morgan Noronha (14)	40
Al-Ameen Abidemi Ahmed (11)	42
Maizie Lois McDonald (12)	43
Salma Ahmed (16)	44
Hannah Golding (14)	45
Zubeida Sadat (11)	46
Aimey Saxon	47
Megan Beavis (15)	48
Mia Demi Steemson (14)	50
Inaaya Naseer (10)	51
Reka Farkas (11)	52
Blenne Emma Abate (9)	53
Anabia Eman (9)	54
Charlotte Collins (7)	55
Maisie Rosetta Moseley (13)	56
Karina Palkowska (11)	57
Haaris Mirzaii (10)	58
Jamie Jackson (15)	59
Isla Stewart (9)	60
Andel Asare (11)	61
Abdulelah Mahmoud Alsabhi (10)	62
Kimberly Alexis Singer (18)	63
Albi Perrott Morter (9)	64
Danyal Rashid (9)	65
Chloe Dojli (11)	66
Hanalee Davies (11)	67
Sukhmani Kaur Sidhu (9)	68
Aafreen Zainab Kashif (15)	69
Alexandra Matei (14)	70
Bentley Oyenjij (9)	71
Tulisa Louise Steady (7)	72
Janya Balian (13)	73
Safaa Mahnoor Hosany (10)	74
Mahveen Ana Chowdhury (8)	75
Kayden Holmes (9)	76
Rola Al-Hassani (11)	77
Katie Alexandra Cleghorn (14)	78
Phoebe Grace Ellis (9)	79
Lily Razok (10)	80
Ellie Doll Ellis (10)	81
Areej Abdul (9)	82
Kairav Ahuja (11)	83
Perla Alegra Petkeviciute (9)	84
Anik Mitra (16)	85
Ann Rabea (11)	86
Hassan Babar	87
Grace Marie Southee (11)	88

Name	No.
Hala Mahmoud Radwan (9)	89
Hayden Clutton (10)	90
Melissa Lynch (11)	91
Chloe Godfrey	92
Cheyenne Jaycee Mary Walsh (11)	93
Hazel Gonsalves (10)	94
Alex Pollard	95
Anushree Nikhil Kaluskar (12)	96
Abeera Aftab (11)	97
Nehimiah Wairia (13)	98
Mia Brownbill	99
Annabelle Rose Brett (7)	100
Lilian Hardill (12)	101
Surya Senthilkumar (12)	102
Mobolajoko Abigael Olanibijuwon (8)	103
Ellie Attwood (9)	104
Ruby-Mae Saunders (9)	105
Amelia Fathulla (9)	106
Sharanya Sonthalia (11)	107
Dominic O'Brien (11)	108
Tess Jacobs (11)	109
Grace Olaoye (11)	110
David Baffour Atuahene Ofosuhene (12)	111
Emily Rose Pettitt (12)	112
Daljit Singh Virk (11)	113
Simra Noor Aziz (8)	114
Kesley Brito	115
Ryan Ashton Ashton Moyo (10)	116
Michael Akintayo Akinwonmi-Pedro (9)	117
Alexander Pagtalunan Church (11)	118
Lola Marshall	119
Aneta Charvatova (10)	120
Aemon Blake Adiz (10)	121
Emaan Ali Khan	122
Megan Powell (12)	123
Kenzie Sarah Jane Avey (8)	124
Miley Goodman (9)	125
Rylan Miguel Longog Medina-Longog (9)	126
Savannah Rose H (10)	127
Muzn Hassan (10)	128
Ruby Jones (9)	129
Jagoda Kramarz (9)	130
Priya Bose (9)	131
Hollie Smith (9)	132
Scarlett Anne Pattinson (10)	133
Zlata Strelkova (9)	134
Houda Mountaser (10)	135
Olivia Poltorak (8)	136
Nia Davies (12)	137
Troie Kannasizam Oranyendu (8)	138
Isabelle Palmer (9)	139
Adina Jashari	140
Lenard Williams (8)	141
DyuthiMohan Tulasi (9)	142
Abeeshana Ariyararatnam (11)	143
Reem Taan (7)	144

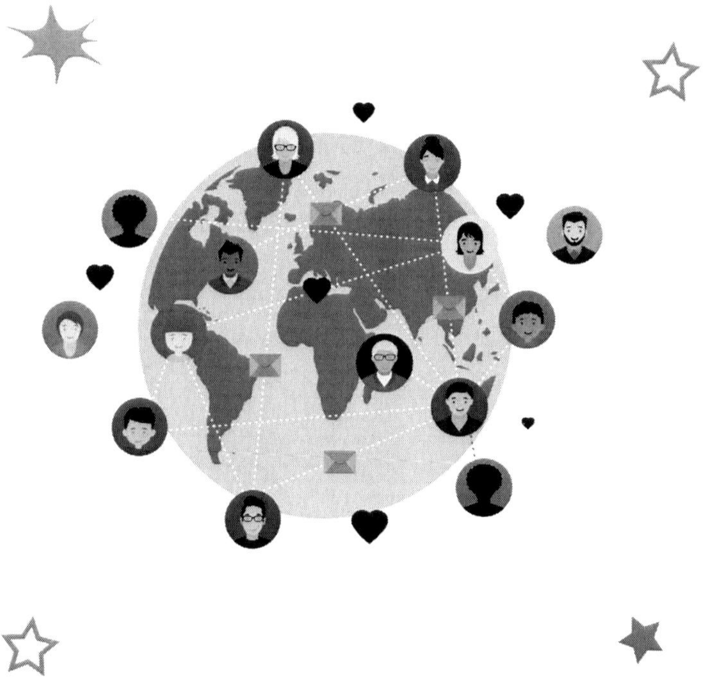

Write To Unite - Together We Stand

My Secret Life

I was sat down on my favourite chair in the house that was in the living room in front of the TV. I took the remote and turned on Good Morning Britain, my daily news. and I was very shocked that there had been a fatal outbreak of COVID-19 in the UK. I knew what that meant. It meant that I had to get to work ASAP because my name is Jacey and I am a nurse that works with the NHS.

Once I had finally arrived at work, everybody was in a huge rush and there was a long queue of people, that were at least two metres apart, waiting to be seen by a doctor... This was going to be a long day.

My first patient was a little girl called Molly, she was very scared. I knew just what to do. I knelt on the floor in front of her and said, "Under all this stuff I'm smiling because I can see you." You see I was wearing a face mask and gloves and other stuff to protect myself from COVID and I knew this could look scary to a little girl.

She looked up at me with her big blue eyes and said, "Are you really?"

"Yes I am," I said. She told me that she didn't feel very good today, her head and tummy were hurting. I took her temperature, it was okay. I examined her and reassured her that I thought she would be okay. She then went back to wait to see the doctor.

A little later I saw her just as she was leaving and she stopped and said, "Thank you for smiling, you made me feel better." This made my day and I went home later smiling knowing that just smiling or knowing someone is smiling at you can make a difference.

Ebony Bushby (11)

An Elfish Assassin

Chapter One: Moon Mist

It was a dark and misty night and the moon was full. The light, indefinite squelch of footsteps in the mud cut the eerie silence of the dark night. Peacefully Mr Owltree slept in his dreadful criminal hideout, blissfully unaware of the undignified death that he was to face tonight. Elvendias the panther slowly slipped into Owltree's open window, Elven crept into the filthy, unsanitary bedroom quietly bent over his head and in the bat of an eyelash Mr Owltree had died an unsatisfactory death. His blood began to seep into the pillow dyeing it a nasty shade of deep red.

"Done, 100 gold in the bag," whispered Elven carefully. Silently she snuck out of the house. Just like that, a major crime chain ended.

Chapter Two: Ironfire

"Hey babe," called Elven.
"Did you do it?" asked Chip.
"Nice to see you too."
"Well?" inquired Chip.
"Yes I did Chip, he had no protection at all."
"Good."
"What's for dinner?"
"Gammon and chips," replied Chip.
"Yum," cried Elven.
"Here you go!" exclaimed Chip.
"Food!" screamed Elven.

After devouring a full plate of steaming gammon and chips, Elven declared she was going to the portal plane. Upon arriving in the portal plane, Elven began to search for the portal to the were-wolf territory to follow up some rumours of a certain dealer.
"The ironfire blades," demanded Elven.
"They don't come cheap," protested the shady dealer. Elven dumped the brown sack of gold on the counter, the dealer's eyes gleamed with greed.
"The ironfire blades and a little info on them please," asked Elven, for the second time.
"Okay," agreed the dealer, taking the sack and in return placing the blades and their enchanted sheath. "Ironfire, the hottest metal on earth, is forged in the human volcanoes. Remains hot after its creation and can cut through virtually anything. There are only two blades in the world and they're right here," said the dealer in something similar to awe.
"Thank you, good day to you sir," said Elven, then punched him in the face, knocking him out cold. "Thanks," Elven said. Grimacing she took back the gold.
After returning to the portal plane, Elven then headed to the vampire lands where she consorted with a vampire princess named Fang. She was fifth in line for the throne and has over ten children but still found time to meet Elven.
"Hey princess," called Elven.
"I told you not to call me that," groaned Fang.
Elven chuckled. "Okay, okay, we have business to attend to."
"Yes we do. Here is my mother's fang as promised, remember to feed it with blood and that it's reusable," explained Fang.

"As my part of the deal I will protect you and your children to the best of my ability during the next war," promised Elven.
"Blood bind yourself," demanded Fang.
"Fine," agreed Elven. A blood bind is an extreme version of a promise, it means that if you break that promise you will become a soulless being not being alive nor dead.
Fang drew a circle around them both in tree sap. "I swear on the blood of my fathers and the pride of my family that I Elvendias Shadow will protect Fang princess of the vampire lands fifth in line to the throne to the best of my ability and skill in the next war," swore Elven.
"In turn I swear on the fangs of my mothers I will do as Elvendias commands in order to protect me and my children," swore Fang. They shook hands to seal it. A sharp pain flooded through Elven`s body as if she were being stabbed with a million swords.
"I'm going home, see you later Fang," said Elven in a small voice as a binding can do a great deal to an elf's strength. Upon arriving home Elven found Chip asleep and collapsed right next to her on the bed.

Chapter Three: Demon's Assassin

"Morning sleepyhead you've been called into a meeting at 12:30 and it's 12:00 now so get up," called Chip cheerily.
"WHAT! Why didn't you wake me up earlier?" screamed Elven frantically pulling on her assassin's uniform.
"Because then it's no fun," chuckled Chip.
"Ugh why are you like this?" Shoving a piece of toast in her mouth, Elven sped out of the door and on to the street all in a blur. Eventually arriving at the Agency, Elven was greeted with a singular man dressed in a black attire consisting of a long formal coat and a suit with a navy blue tie.

"Elvendias, I was waiting for you," stated the man calmly.
"Yes sir, sorry sir," apologised Elven
"A new task has arisen should you choose to complete it. It is to take out Savage," he said.
"Accept whether fatal or not," pledged Elven.
"The file shall arrive through post tomorrow," he declared.
Elven walked the strangely desolate streets, passing the usually crowded, library. "That's odd," she said to herself. A deep, malicious cackle rang through her head. Elven broke out into a run, now speeding along the pavement. The same deep voice spoke: "You can't escape little elf." Elven tripped on an upturned slab. "Mwha ha ha," it cackled.
"Who are you?" Elven shouted at the sky.
"Aww shouldn't you know that? I am your mission after all," the voice said.
"Savage," muttered Elven. "How did you know that?"
"I know everything," he taunted
A loud thud and a violent pain hit Elven's head. Everything went blurry.
Gasping, the next thing she knew she was lying in a hospital bed. "What happened? Where am I?" asked Elven in a panic.
"You're in the hospital Elven, you passed out in the middle of the busy streets and you cracked the back of your head open," explained Chip.
"What!? Busy? The streets were empty and Savage was cackling and taunting me," said Elven in shock.
"Who is Savage?" asked Chip.
"He is my new target."
"It could be, anyway you've been in here for two days and you're getting discharged tonight."
"Okay good, I need to train longer and harder."

"No Elven you are just coming out from stitches there is no way I'm letting you go to the training centre."
"Yes I am and you can't stop me," said Elven.
"Miss Chip Walker may you please leave," asked the doctor.
"Yes mam," obeyed Chip.
"Miss Elvendias Shadow you can leave now," said the doctor whilst she unhooked her from the machines. Then the doctor handed her the clothes she was wearing when she fell.

Chapter Four: Attack
"Hey babe lets go home," Elven said.
"Okay," Chip replied coldly. After arriving home Chip went to the toilet as Elven got changed into her sportswear. "Hey please Elven you can't strain yourself like this, if you push your body too hard you'll break it," Chip told Elven.
"You know I'm still gonna go," replied Elven.
"Don't make me fight you Elven," threatened Chip. A huge blast of cord wrapped themselves around Elven's hand and feet then constricted her limbs together.
"Urgh," groaned Elven, "let me go!" she shouted.
"No," said Chip, tears streaming down her face. "It's for your own good."
Elven began crying as well. "I'm so sorry, I just wanted to protect our family from this mess that I got us into," bawled Elven.

To be continued...

Lauren Nkosephayo Johnson

Relief

Hello. Relief can come in a form of joy and is hard to reach. Coronavirus has made it hard for people to see the silver lining in the dark cloud so I have written this. You may have experienced relief before and that is amazing! If not, this is for you. I am here to confirm that the purpose of this letter is not for any worries to come over you, but for relief to pass through you. So I suggest you please remain calm.

I just want to say that I am so appreciative for the people around me and protecting me. No, I am not talking about the NHS, but all the key workers out there! I'm talking about the doctors, nurses and midwives, care workers and teachers, cleaners, shop sellers and keepers, court staff, journalist, delivery workers, firefighters and transport workers(sorry if I missed any). They are wonderful and if this was a fairy tale, we would be damsels in distress and they would be the knights in shining armour.

Also, I've gotta be real. We are also one of the reasons we are still alive. We are protecting ourselves by staying at home, staying healthy and making sure that we work on our mental health as well as our physical health. And we need to keep it up. So please, take my advice and the health experts and do your part. Plus, they don't say 'At the end of every dark tunnel comes a rainbow' for nothing. So please do stay positive and friendly in this situation. I hope we come out of COVID-19 more knowledgeable, responsible and definitely more clean. Thank you!

Umu Hawa Kemokai (10)

Believe!

Once there was a boy called Jim. He was an ordinary child. Although he may look normal there was something very peculiar about him. Jim was interested in books of superheroes and they used to pick and bully him because of this. He always dreamt his superhero toys would come to life.

One day (like every other day) he came home crying and went straight to his room like always. His tears gushed out like a waterfall as he stared into the mirror. "Why does nobody like me? Why do I have to be like this?" he questioned himself.

He looked at his toys and it looked like it was hugging him. He knew it was not real and does not believe this. He didn't want to be even weirder by letting his imagination get to him. They even cheered for him, but he still did not believe that this was real.

As the day went on Jim went to sleep. His hopeless tears soaked his pillow wishing he was like everybody else. Suddenly as he went to sleep the toys came alive! Their eyes glistened in the moonlight and arose from their statue figures. They'd had enough of their usual night which is to play chess; they were bored of that. So, the king of all superheroes demanded to leave. This was Jim's favourite toy, he had a figure of a bodybuilder and skin like a bronzed god. His tall body was draped with a blue and green costume and always had a smile on his face.

After days of planning, they finally had a winning plan. This was the night. They escaped the house and it was a rough time in all the rain and the storms but finally they reached their destination - the glorious arcade!

The machines were calling their names as the vibrant lights flashed excitedly. It was like heaven to them, but the only problem was, it was locked. This did not stop the toys from getting what they always wanted and was an easy job for the superheroes. Everybody had a job to do, no one was left apart and they all stuck together.

I bet you're asking how they get inside the arcade. They stole the key from the janitor and unlocked the back door. Pretty easy right?

As they were enjoying their playing, they heard a bang. Their electrical hearts were beating erratically. It was the owner looking for the keys. What were they going to do? Was their plan not good enough? They had to think of something quickly or else they would be no more. They decided to hide the key in the basement, but it was too dark, and they could not reach the lights. "Quick! to the toilets," the boss said as they flushed the keys down and jumped out the window and managed to reach home.

What an adventure that was! But what really mattered now was Jim. They had to prove to him they were alive and are going to protect him because he was an amazing owner to them. Although he may seem like a fool to his classmates and parents his toys knew they had to show him some gratitude.

The next morning, Jim was ready for another day of battering, bullying and complete disgust. I guess he was immune to the pain and found it completely normal now.

To his surprise, as he was getting ready for school, he saw a card on his desk. A beautiful superhero card which made his sombre face fill bright with light. He felt bad for not believing in his toys but promised never to stop being himself. Being weird is unique and unique is special. You may seem peculiar to others but a great friend to others.

Yasaa Uddin (10)

Write To Unite

This is a story about COVID-19 and how it's affecting us.

There was a girl that liked going outside a lot but one day she went to see what was on TV, she saw the government talking about the horrible, scary illness called COVID-19 but it wasn't that bad at the time.

The next day she went to school. Out of nowhere her teacher said, "We're going to do a test today because of the illness." The girl wasn't ready for these tests, she was so worried but so mad on the inside.

On Friday was her last day, she was so sad to say goodbye to her amazing, loving, caring friends but all of a sudden she remembered about her family then she took things seriously, she was so sad.

The next day, she saw people playing out with their neighbours so she asked her mom, "Why are people playing out?"

Her mom responded, "Well they are being naughty." The girl really wanted to play as well.

Every time she heard a knock on the door, all she saw was a bag full of goodies from Nanny. She wished that all this was over since it was making her family sad.

When she heard a helicopter she raced outside to look up to see if it's the army one, she just stared at it realising this was actually happening.

She says in her head *it's going to be over very soon you've just gotta stay at home and believe everything is going to be okay real soon!*

Lacey-Jai Stokes (10)

Thank You NHS!

My name is Anhaar Ishak and I'm eleven years old and today I'm writing about the NHS, and how they risk their lives to help and support us on this dangerous mission. The Coronavirus, which is a very deadly disease, is killing many people and is passing around countries but still the NHS carries on the important job of making sure we are safe. I may not know much, but right now all I'm thinking about is how the NHS is coping in this situation.

This virus is stopping kids from education and enjoying their right to play. In Unicef, Article 31 says 'Every child has the right to relax and play' but this article is being neglected. We can't play properly when we're stuck inside. Not only this but it is also making the NHS work at this time, while they should be home caring for themselves. This virus now has become a big deal. We should all thank the NHS for making sure we are healthy. Should the NHS work at this time of suffering, or should they be home making sure they don't catch anything?

For all those reasons, the NHS deserves a pay rise. They are working hard and deserve more than just a thank you and a round of applause. Not only the NHS but all those people who are still working. But a special thank you to the bin men that are still taking our rubbish and making sure we have a clean environment. This is why all these job working people deserve a higher pay rise. Why should these particular people carry on working and risk their lives for our country? The bin people come every week and clean up the mess they never made, they come here at this time and help us! And all we do is sit home and sulk.

We should all try better and not stay like this. The least we can do is put our rubbish in the right bin, the plastic and cartons should be placed separately and everything must be in order.

But to this day, no one wants to give a real thank you! Our lives have become more serious because now not only can we not leave our houses but carry on a normal day. Boris Johnson thanked the NHS but is that all? Shouldn't we do more to support them?

Honestly, I think we should start making sure we do what's right for our country, our future, our lives. We haven't done much to save our country. The CoronaVirus won't leave if we don't try to stop it from spreading. Let's give an awesome thank you to the NHS and all key workers. I'm happy that in my country people aren't giving up.

Boris Johnson if you get a chance to read this, then you will understand that we haven't given up yet. We will fight till the very end until the NHS gets all the things they need to carry on their good work. Carry on fighting for us! We will support you till the very end, don't give up. Stay home, stay safe, save the NHS!

We can see, that the NHS and key workers need more attention. If it wasn't for them the UK would have fallen apart. They are helping us at a time that people are so scared to leave their houses. We're at home, they're in work. We are relaxing, they are trying hard. Why should they do all this? And we do so less! I just wanted to say thank you for helping me and my country!

Anhaar Ishak (11)

How The World Defeated Coronavirus

It was the year 2020 and on Planet Earth, a silent assassin was lurking in the darkness... Coronavirus. It had taken away more lives from us than the plague, and it was still going. There was only one last hope for Planet Earth, Geoff Gandoor, the best scientist in the world... no... the UNIVERSE had ever seen in millenniums. At the young age of fifteen, he already knew more about science than fully-fledged scientists and at twenty-three he achieved:

A master's degree in science

Found the treatment for cancer

And much more!

But this, if he found out this, this would be the highlight of his career, he could see it now; if he found the cure for this new-fangled disease, he could sell it for millions, or trillions, or even... octillions! The Queen might even knight him and make him into a Sir... 'Sir Geoff Gandoor', it sounded so posh, so royal, so kinglike.

Ahh, then, "Yawnnnnnnn!!!!!!!" Geoff woke up. "What is the time?" he thought to himself. "AAAHHHHH!" It was 9am, "I am an hour late for my first day at work!" he shouted.

He quickly got dressed and drove to his new workplace, the RSSMD (The Royal Society of Science and Medical Discoveries). What a joy it was to be in there! He was so happy that he was practically levitating in the air.

He went in and everyone was as busy as bees! It wasn't just Geoff who wanted to figure out the antidote for Coronavirus, it was everybody! So, he had to work just as hard as anyone else.

For hours on end, Geoff worked tirelessly in his workspace, and then, after a long time (and a lot of failed treatments) he collected together twenty-three hours of work and made his final antidote. He called it: *The Corona Killer*. He gave *Corona Killer* to Mary Lopkins, The First Minister of Vaccines and Antidotes, and after that, waited impatiently for the results, while hopping up and down the lab, until, the moment came...

"Geoff Gandoor," she said in a stupendously posh voice, "you have successfully created the treatment for this pandemic, well done". Geoff was over the moon as soon as he heard the news, he would be a trillionaire!!! "I think you need to get to work now," said Mary, still in a stupendously posh voice.

"Hooray!"

Moral:

Remember, even when it feels like that it will never end, it will always stop. Tough times cannot last forever, and if you always stay positive and keep on going, it will always work out in the end.

Rajan Kumar (11)

A Virus

A virus. This seems scary to us all especially the one we are facing at the moment. But, that does not mean that we just sit around and do nothing. This virus does not give us the right to have any type of excuse to be lazy. This virus is keeping us stuck at home. But my question is, is being stuck at home necessarily a bad thing?

While we are at home we should not be lazy in fact we should be active. A healthy body equals a healthy mind. So, exercise and keep yourself satisfied. We must find ways to have fun. So if that means getting up during your free time and talking to someone, do it!

I know some of you are on your phones, laptops and other devices while lying in your bed. Technology has taken over the human mind and has stopped people from going outside and enjoying the fresh air. This is a time that we should be spending with our family and not with our devices. Who said gardens are not available for you anymore? Have fun outside. We all have to face the real world some day.

Books are a lovely way to calm yourself and interest you. Maybe try something new for a change? Sometimes a little adventure can do us all some good. Throw your self out there (not literally).

People are nervous and we all know that but think about the positive side to this. If you have wanted to sit down in your room and do something for while but you couldn't because you had no spare time, well this is your chance. If you are really bored try to call a friend and maybe do some school work with them or sit down and have a chat. Learn how to cook something with your mum or dad.

Most importantly, do not spread hate because we do not need to worry about any hate during this time.

Just remember none of us are alone here. We will all get through this. Be thankful that we have amazing people out there trying to find a cure to this virus. A virus cannot stop us from doing things that we love and spending time with people who we love. A virus can not stop us from smiling. A virus is not worth our misery.

Miar Abouarghoub (12)

We Are In This Together!

Sadness has taken over our lives,
We don't know who survives,
But we must remember,
Things other than this crisis from December,
Just like the beautiful weather,
We are in this together!

Seeing the sun rise in the morning,
Thinking about someone's death and another's mourning,
Making, baking, eating, cleaning,
Thinking about life's meaning,
Playing games and having fun,
Thinking about what's happening to everyone,
Looking out of the window at the weather,
Remembering, we are in this together!

Remembering the past seems like a blur,
When happy we were,
The times we would meet our family,
But now they are gone, turning into a fantasy,
The times we went to school to learn,
But now that's gone, while we wait for those days to return,
The times we had no worries and were relieved,
But now that's gone, leaving us deceived,
We can still remember, without having to gather,
That we are in this together!

We need to stay two metres away,
From everyone, every day,
Happy birthday we recite,
While washing our hands day and night,
Wearing masks when we go outside,
Escaping from everyone, trying to hide,
Putting on sanitizer everywhere,
Wiping out a single tear,
Trying hard not to cry,
Cursing our fate, asking why,
But we need to see the bright side,
And forget about all the times we have cried,
Put our worries away and look at the wonderful weather,
Because we are in this together!

From our loved ones, we are apart,
But they will always be in our heart,
Including the times we spent,
With all the warmth and content,
We need to remember those and stay well,
As in the future, we all have a story to tell,
And we need to think that this is all for the better,
That this is an amazing adventure,
We are in this together!

Himani Juneja (12)

From Despair Comes Hope

In 2019, the Coronavirus started,
Now it's 2020 and it still hasn't departed.

It started in China, the city of Wuhan,
Where all the unfortunate deaths had begun.

Everyone started to wear masks on their faces,
As COVID-19 produced many more cases.

Soon the virus was described as a pandemic,
Finding out more was the job of academics.

They started work on creating a vaccination,
That would take years! Was the interpretation.

It started to spread all over the world,
Like wildfire as some had foretold.

Quickly, it came to Europe, more so Italy,
Where the cases soared fast, frighteningly.

The country went into lockdown – all was at a halt.
People stayed at home, wondering if they're at fault.

Now people were buying loo rolls and sanitisers in the UK,
Wondering how this would affect us – will things be okay?

Many were queuing outside supermarkets - buying selfishly,
Whilst others concerned for the vulnerable - helped selflessly.

Eventually, Boris Johnson concluded it's time to lockdown,
Schools, pubs, cinemas...all unessential was shut down.

Protect the NHS was his ultimate message,
Keep well, stay safe, stay at home he encouraged.

Children stayed active at home doing PE with Joe Wicks,
Homeschooling a challenge as kids get up to their usual tricks.

The NHS working tirelessly, trying to keep the cases at bay,
Public showing gratitude as they clap on the eve of every Thursday.

Nobody knows how long this will last,
Let's hope, have faith – soon it'll be the past!

Aaminah Moosa (11)

Life In Quarantine

Every day I will fight,
Life is getting quite tight,
I can't go on my bike,
Feel like taking a hike.
Say hello on Skype
What else should I type?
Darker than the light
Soon I feel a bite
Sleeping through the night
Now I feel alive
I know it's right
I will survive
Through every fight
What will suffice?

Realised it was a game
I have got the fame
And now I can claim
This awesome name
You should be ashamed
You got defamed
Do you like my forename?

Stay away from me
I have a degree
Don't touch my key

Write To Unite - Together We Stand

On that, I agree
Who is that I see?
Falling on me
I would like to guarantee
If he's here for groceries

Stay at home
In your protected dome
Go on chrome
Eat a cone
Don't go to Rome
Wash yourself with foam
You can roam
Inside your home
Let me here an ohm
Move around your gnomes
Go outside alone
On your own
Sit on a throne
OMG you've grown
Watch Home Alone
Or Sherlock Holmes
Step into a new biome
Stare into the unknown
Please don't let me scold
Stay away from the old
Stay in your stronghold
I'm in quarantine

I've been making memes
I have schemes
I will dream
Watched some scenes
On the TV screen
Applied the cream
I have good genes
Today I ate beans
I can't load teams
Also I saw steam
I can see your regime
I know the marines
I hope human beings
Can find a vaccine
Why are you so mean?
We are all in quarantine.

Ansh Bahl

Suri And Kara's Exciting Adventure To Planet Krypton!

Dear diary,

Yesterday, I had the best and exciting day of my life. This is what happened. I woke up very excited because I was going on a trip to Planet Krypton with my best friend Kara, who is one of the most famous superheroes, Supergirl! I knew it was going to be fun. I hopped onto Kara's back holding our bags and she flew to Planet Krypton.

When we landed, Kara told me that Planet Krypton was where she first discovered her powers, so I thought that I might get my powers here. My mum told me that my powers would have something to do with crushing. We went into our penthouse and unpacked when a loud crash occurred and Kara used her super hearing to hear the Doomsday Creator (the baddest villain in the world) saying that he was going to destroy Planet Krypton (with the people inside it). Kara told me what he said and also told me that he has her weakness called the Green Orb. We quickly went to him. I used my mind to crush a Coke can on the floor and it happened. Kara used her laser eyes to zap his armour off. I crushed his MegaEvilMobile so he wouldn't escape. He took the Green Orb out from his hood. I told Kara to hide behind the van so she wouldn't get affected. I crushed the Orb so it wouldn't hurt her. Kara zapped him and I crushed him until he couldn't move. Finally we turned him in, celebrated and went back home.

Suraiya Rahman (12)

There Is Still Hope

I sit there, all curled up not wanting to move or interact with anything. The dim-lit room surrounding me, messy and cold. I am alone, nobody is with me. My family has been spending days in the hospital while I have been spending days stuck in my room. I see the window next to me, flushing in gusts of freshened air into a compact and stuffy room.

All I have been doing these past few days are eating, sleeping and that's all. I have no hope for myself. As the wind enters my room, I gather all my energy to stand up and try shutting it. My hands clasp onto the frames of the dirty and tiny window and use full force to try shutting them. Something prevents me from doing so. A strength stronger than mine. Something preventing me from interacting with the outdoors, life. I try to hold back and close it, but that strength lingers there, telling me to stop from keeping away from it.

Hope lingers there, overpowering my hopelessness and telling me indirectly, 'I'm still here.' There is still hope for a change. Hope that will guide us through this rough time and help us to stay lively. It will prepare us for the future.

With hope, there will be a better future. With hope, we will all courageously fight the pandemic. We will beat it and we will fight together. All we need is hope for a better future. Don't think that hope doesn't exist at this time.

Just know that all that is going on is temporary and we will soon find a way out.
Hope still exists.
Hope is there for us all, and we will fight for our way with it.

Alina Ahmed (13)

The Shy Superhero

Once upon a time there was a superhero that lived in a small town called Eguia.
The superhero's name was Triggerman, he wore a bright green costume and a green face mask. Triggerman was very shy because he didn't believe in himself. However Triggerman never gave up, he always tried his best. He tried not to show people he was nervous, so he tried to avoid talking to people, but this made him lonely. Triggerman wanted to make friends and have people to talk to. Triggerman would normally be assigned about 2-3 missions a day. However this time Triggerman was not given a mission. He searched all day for villains but he just couldn't find any and he was getting bored. All he could see was people walking by, he decided instead of looking for villains, he would go and look for friends instead. He saw an old lady struggling to carry shopping, Triggerman decided to go and help her. He carried her shopping home for her, the lady was grateful and made a fuss of him. Soon a small crowd was forming, everyone wanted to know who triggerman was. Instead of flying away like he would normally, Triggerman stayed and spoke to the people, they were all very kind and triggerman realised that they could be friends. He didn't feel lonely anymore and felt happier. Triggerman realised that no matter what, no one should feel lonely.

Eesa Raza (7)

Life Being In Lockdown

It was a cold but sunny day on Monday 23rd March 2020. We were told the UK is going into lockdown, which meant I wouldn't be returning to school and seeing my friends and family.

As days went by, it got stricter and stricter as many people did not listen to the UK Prime Minister. Food places closed, Along with pubs and most shops. My mum and dad kept me and my little sister safe but also busy as I am doing a lot of homeschooling, Learning new things and mostly understanding the importance of why we are in lockdown. I can only play in my garden and go for a walk around the block on my estate.

It is such a horrible feeling, I just want things to go back to how they used to be and for all this to go away. I want to enjoy the weather and to be able to see my grandparents. Me and my sister miss their hugs and kisses and we miss them a lot. It is not the same seeing them on facetime, not being able to touch or talk to them in person. As each day goes by we are still doing things at home, still doing things alone. The sun is shining and we cannot even go to the park to play or go and feed the ducks, this is not a very nice feeling. Please listen to the Prime Minister, please stay home and be safe. We will have to protect everyone. We all need this to go away.

Savannah Banger (5)

Our Home

Hearing the joyful screams of children playing
The utter jubilation filling up inside of us
The voices of adults speaking
This is our home

The children enjoying outside in the garden
The lovely gentle breeze brushing against our face
The sunshine brightness made us happy
This is our home

The coughs of the devil infesting us
Screams of children, slowly vanishing
The corrupted voices of adult started to fade
This is our home

Constant online streaming masses being hosted
The continuous prayers being said
The meditation reflections being thought
This is our home

People are dying in the hospital where being filmed
Millions of people are infested and hungry
Front liners, the heroes struggle to fight the killer virus
Children look sad, adult tears dripping on their face

This is our home
The leaders, the people your love and care
Never stop believing, unite each other

There is hope, pray for God's Blessings
Be kind, be strong and do not give up
Give your hands to others, the Earth, our home.

Angelo Eleazar Gallaza (12)

Being United

During this apocalyptic time, it is important to be united. This Coronavirus pandemic has put us to the test by showing its devastating consequences. Alone we are ordinary, but together we are incredible, that is why we ask you to: "Stay home, protect the NHS and save lives."
It hurts us, the fact that people are losing their loved ones. It is not easy to cope with such stress, as this virus is taking its daily tolls, dragging our stress levels to the limits; the pain that you are in today is the strength you will need to build up for the next day.
We will defeat this invisible killer! We will experience better days, as we deserve.
Our good survives anything except that misunderstanding in us. We need to understand that ditching hope is only making matters worse. Let's create this ripple of hope by supporting each other. Our behaviour is crucial to beat this virus, our potential is endless!
We thank all the NHS and care home staff working on the front line. We also thank all key workers for their commitment to keeping the society moving forward.
Together we can do anything.

Patricia Nsue Nvomo (12)

Write To Unite - Together We Stand

Coronavirus Will Not Win!

I want to leave you all knowing,
That our human legacy will just keep growing.
With countries on lockdown and some are writhing in pain,
The disease's intentions will soon be slain.
I am proud of all recoveries,
So there is no place for any anxieties.
Whatever decides to come our way,
We will soon demolish it some day.
We all have a role to play, I can tell,
As we try to bid the virus farewell.
We can restore the peace that has once been,
Coronavirus will just never win!
We might think it's something bizarre,
But in the end, we will shout HUZZAH!
Nothing can wipe out human life,
Even though over time, diseases have caused a bit of strife.
We have been around for 200,000 years,
Better make it count to get rid of our fears.
Living our lives is not a sin,
Get rid of Coronavirus because it will just never win!
Washing hands is the main objective,
Soon you'll see how much it's been effective.
Social distancing is something annoying,
Hard to do, but the end results will not be terrifying.

Masa Barakat (12)

Pandemic

In a time of despair and fear we must come together, Because only together can we beat this national pandemic. I look up to with admiration and respect the people who are putting their lives on the line for us. To the NHS, shopkeepers, carers all the way to the postman - all the key workers - you are the people who keep this country running. With all my heart I thank you because without you this country wouldn't be running the way it is.

I know many of us have lost our loved ones and I can't imagine how much pain you're going through, I hope those who have left us due to this national trauma have found peace and left in a better place, and I hope those who have lost let the light back in. I know it's hard and the pain may be unbearable but I hope you can get through your agonising pain. I hope this danger comes to an end so that no one else will lose their loved ones, so no one else will have to bear insufferable pain which many have gone through. I hope that this national pandemic comes to an end I hope we can all come together and be stronger than ever.

Esha Furrukh (13)

Together To Make It Bright

This thing that's happening in the world right now
It's frightening and scary, it's time to be brave but how?
We must help one another and help our country
This is our chance to write our future story.
We miss the things we used to do
But now is the time to learn things that are new.
We can draw and paint and cook a cake or two
No need to sleep all day, go out and exercise to stop you feeling blue.
We can still have fun every day,
even if we can't go to our friends to play.
I'm having fun with my family and pets,
we follow the rules, keeping away the virus' threats.
Be brave and be honest, and say if your scared,
Just know our country and heroes are well prepared.
Paint a rainbow and paint it bright,
As a sign to show hope and bring the end closer in sight.
For now this is our world but stay as strong as you can,
for these hopes and wishes will help every man.
Clap for every hero on a Thursday night,
and fight for a future we can have that is bright.

Jorja Lacey Morgan (10)

Unity Through A Crisis

The streets lie empty,
Where there should be plenty.
The supermarket shelves vacant,
We just need to be patient!

Unity, unity holding us together,
Let's stay strong and end this forever,
"We can do this" is what I believe
And if we keep going, I know we can achieve!

NHS, NHS, you are just the best!
If you weren't here, we'd be a mess,
You are doing all you can,
Even though we don't have a plan.

Unity, unity holding us together,
Let's stay strong and end this forever,
"We can do this" is what I believe
And if we keep going, I know we can achieve!

Hygiene, hygiene let's keep clean,
End this virus and not get in-between,
We stand distant, we wear gloves, and we wear masks
To help stop the virus from spreading fast!

Unity, unity holding us together,
Let's stay strong and end this forever,
"We can do this" is what I believe
And if we keep going, I know we can achieve!

Jamil Ladha (12)

Let Us Fight COVID-19

In this crisis of worldwide quarantine
We are all out of routine
But nature made us realise
How mean we have been

We never heard the birds sing
Or see the bright blue skies
Now locked inside
We realise how we stopped
The sphere to breathe outside

If we realise our mistake
There is a journey we can retake
And reclaim the Earth
To allow its rebirth
Because united we stand
And divided we fail
We are all scared
But really we shouldn't be compared
We're worried if life will be the same
But how will we predict the game
There is bound to be fight
And we will show COVID-19 who really is right

I see love in the air
But nothing seems fair

Stay at home
Remember to comb
We need to stay united
Together we can fight it

Let's stick together
And fight it forever
You play your part
And soon you can push
Your own cart

Let's fight it once and for all
Then no one will fall.

Saachi Jawa (10)

Paradisum

A plague, thou were ravaged by,
Even the mighty iron birds ceased to fly,
Only worsening is this situation dire,
Will mine life end fighting this fire,

All hope was lost,
Great Empires bitten by the frost,
Havoc the plague wreaked,
With blood, houses were streaked,

Alas, from the darkness, came through, a light,
Ended not had our fight,
But opened were our eyes,
Heard were our humble cries,

Nature we saw thrive,
It was the planets chance to survive,
The sun shone radiantly through the clouds,
The animals came, far from the madding crowd,

People were far apart yet close,
Understood, was the path we chose,
Thought of were others,
Remembered were sisters and brothers,

Our death the plague hath prevented,
A new way of life was consented,
A curse this was not,

A blessing brought,
A new world we will be given,
Evil was driven,
We have no reason to be glum,
We have been given a paradisum.

Morgan Noronha (14)

Be Hopeful!

As we all know, COVID-19 is a big problem for everyone. However, the way we can feel positive about this is by following rules stated by the government, staying at home and protecting the NHS. This will enable us to feel safe and allow us to acknowledge the fact that we know that everything in general is going at a monitored pace as normal.

People are dying every now and then, but it has not happened to you and that is what matters most. Whatever has been done can't be undone and after COVID-19 we will start monitoring our hygiene like we were supposed to, even before the virus started.

All is not lost, we can still help others by giving people what we have, donating to charities and making sure that we obey rules made by the government. In that way we are keeping ourselves and other people safe.

If we all keep calm and have hope, there is nothing to worry about and the virus will clear shortly.

Al-Ameen Abidemi Ahmed (11)

Let's Spread Some Positivity!

At the moment times seem hard. We are all stuck inside and sometimes we can get bored. However, we all need to stay inside because it will help not just us but everyone! Everyone who is currently staying inside are doing a fantastic thing because by staying inside, you are saving lives. At this time, we also need to take time to think about our key workers whose work sometimes gets overlooked and this is the time that all of our key workers have to work their hardest to keep our country running.

From now on, all of the key workers should get the respect and appreciation that they deserve from helping us through this time and they should be so proud of themselves forever for all of the different things they have done for us and they all try their hardest to help people.

All of us will want to go outside, but just remember why we are inside and what could happen if we went outside. Everyone is doing an amazing job and soon we will be able to do things that we love again! Thank you for reading! Stay at home!

Maizie Lois McDonald (12)

The Wildlife Make A Return

The air was purer, the seas clearer... in fact, the streets seemed empty but they were actually secretly full of all the wildlife that had returned since humans went into lockdown. They were the second generation of creatures and could last forever; you can't see most of the wildlife but you feel something is there. What does this mean?

Days went past... Until one day, a half-human and half-wolf hybrid transformed completely from a human to animal. She must have known wildlife was taking over, sensing them from miles away. She was the only human (well hybrid) to know what was happening. The animals were careful when humans were around. They stayed in a place nobody knew of.

You could nature making a return. The green branches of the trees were growing over the buildings and flowers were pushing their way through the cracks in the tarmac of the roads... no one could have ever imagined this - wildlife having its dream life. But how long will it last?

Salma Ahmed (16)

A Normal Day In Quarantine

I went into the kitchen to ask someone what to eat. I didn't ask the freezer because everything he says always chills me to the bone.
I decided to ask the hoover but he just told me to eat dust and leave him alone.
I moved on to the washing machine but she simply told me washing powder is the cure to all her hunger.
The cupboard spat pans at me so I left her alone and the microwave told me I was pushing his buttons and he was losing patience.
The biscuit jar held nothing enticing and the sugar turned out to be salt.
The chair I was sat on told me to stop squashing him and the table told me to rest my plate on her.
The crockery smashed when I asked them what I should eat and the straws told me to suck up my inner courage.
I left the kitchen and plodded up the stairs which told me to stop kicking them and flopped onto my bed which groaned and creaked in pain and fell asleep.
Just another normal day in quarantine...

Hannah Golding (14)

Coronavirus Pandemic

C alm down, don't panic.
O nly stay indoors to end the pandemic.
R espect the front line heroes.
O ur help by staying indoors can drop the number to zero.
N HS is under a lot of pressure.
A nd we are the ones who can relieve the pressure.
V olunteer for those in need and vulnerable.
I can volunteer, you can volunteer.
R oaming around spreads the virus.
U se of home can bring the virus to a minus.
S tay home, protect the NHS, save lives.

P eople are dying in dozens.
A ll are losing their love ones including cousins.
N ations are in fear.
D on't go out, make it clear.
E nd the pandemic.
M ake sure you are safe during this pandemic.
I can protect the NHS, you can protect the NHS, we all can protect our NHS.
C alm down, don't panic.

Zubeida Sadat (11)

A Thank You

During this dreadful and difficult time,
With the nightmare of a pandemic spreading,
We should all say thankyou to our heroes,
A thank you to everyone they're saving!

Say a thank you to our retail workers,
For providing essentials we need to survive.
And to our schools and teaching staff,
For giving us the learning we need to thrive!

Say a thank you to our postwomen and postmen,
For keeping us all in touch.
And to our warehouse workers and delivery drivers,
For stocking or shelves, it's needed much!

And say a thank you to our police and fire service,
Allowing us all to keep well and protected
And to our bin men cleaning our streets,
You really are all respected!

But most importantly, a thank you to our NHS,
For saving our lives and being brave!
Keep doing what your Britain.
Keep us alive, and be behaved.

Aimey Saxon

We Will Beat This Virus

It was like any other day,
The 17th of November,
But what started with a cough
Became a day to remember...

As fast as the news,
A virus spread,
And as numbers grew,
So did our dread.

As quick as a wink
It's 2020
Shoppers start to riot
Toilet paper aisles... empty?

School's out, shops out, taxis and your bus,
Every single thing is out,
Everything, but us...

Everywhere's a ghost town,
Nobody in the streets
Nobody roams,
Can't leave our homes,
Too scared to leave the sheets!

At hard times like these,
Everyone is frightened...

But if we all work together
Our situation will brighten

People will suffer, and times may get tougher,
But with our strong government,
And our NHS, tireless,
All together
We will beat this virus!

Megan Beavis (15)

A Brighter World

Hello, my name is Mia Steemson. I'm here to spread some light during this time of danger and the fear of the unknown.

The world a once free, positive and nutritious place has recently fallen and is being oppressed by this dangerous, alarming virus. Although, many might be worried, distressed and apprehensive towards this life-changing turn of events, we all must stay hopeful yet safe. The darkness may cloud our sense of desire, however we have to hold on to the light. As not only a sovereign country should we band together, but as members of a community and a family.

COVID-19 has forced us into isolation but our confident, incontrovertible attitude will send the country not only into the future, but thriving for greatness.

Spread hope not fear. Love not hate. Show this virus that we are strong, and can restore the world to the once content place it was.

Thank you for listening and I hope everyone is safe.

Mia Demi Steemson (14)

Let's Be One Against COVID-19

Dear Nation

I am writing this letter to hopefully lift your spirits up about this catastrophe called COVID-19. This is not the end of this horrible time just the beginning, but it will end, there is always a light at the end of the tunnel. Self-isolation does not mean no contact with loved ones, technology has become advanced so there are other ways to contact your loved ones.

I am off school and I am homeschooling at the moment, as the days go by, I start to miss my friends more and more, but I know that this is for the better. It is normal to miss people who you are always around even people who you don't get along with. Remember it will end soon and you will be able to reunite with your friends and family. I am happy that I can sleep in and go to bed a bit later. My mum lets me have some extra treats.

We need to stay united and fight this virus together as one. Stay home. Stay safe. Save lives.

Inaaya Naseer (10)

The Great Mysterious Candyland Portal

Once on a warm summer's day, a girl called Ally lived in a city called Liverpool in England. Then, one day, she woke up from a good night sleep and went to do her morning routine as usual but something peculiar happened. Ally went back to her bedroom and found a magical portal. It said 'Portal to Candyland'.

Later, she thought how amazing it would be to be inside Candyland. As she went inside everything was gorgeous. There was candy and sugar everywhere, even a unicorn and a monster were arguing about whose land it is. A minute later, Ally ran towards them and told them, "Maybe try sharing the land and stop fighting!"

After that they said, "No!" but Ally kept on saying, "Just try!" and finally they agreed but still didn't like the idea. So Ally set a plan which was to give both of them a piece of candy. They both liked the candy and all became best friends.

Reka Farkas (11)

Why?

For the first time in my life the world didn't make sense,
All this talk about staying safe,
It bombards you a lot, don't you think?
For ages I sat down,
Wondered. Pondered,
Was this ever going to go away?
Was it going to change people forever?
Was it going to put people in rage?
Try as I might,
It was no use I couldn't get it right!
Then...
Boom! I had got it!
This virus, it wasn't a virus, it was a teacher!
This particular teacher was teaching us to learn from our mistakes,
To stop history repeating itself,
To try to stop putting our lives at stake,
But most of usdidn't listen,
So the teacher got really mad,
The teacher turned bad,
The teacher did not care now,
Why would they?
They had given us a chance,
Anyway that's what I think but it's really up to you...

Blenne Emma Abate (9)

You And Me

You and me,
Me and you,
This is like a happy dream,
Now we're in danger and it will go away soon but there's no need to feel agitated feel like you're a moon!
Imagine your smelling flowers underneath bowers singing in glorious tunes!

Feel like you're dancing while you're actually prancing and your fears will go away soon,

You and me,
Me and you,
I'll see your other friends maybe so soon,

Now let's have some adventures inside because we can't go outside and let's do mischief until it's noon!

I hope Mum won't mind if we start licking on lily coloured lollipops until it's the night-time!

Now let's forget about lockdown goals because there won't make you feel any happier, and let's have some strength in us and we'll succeed in this terrible process!

Anabia Eman (9)

Pets During Coronavirus

One morning, Daisy the Poodle woke up and ran into her owners' bedroom. She licked their faces and got them up to start the day. Daisy's owner let her outside so she could talk to her friends through the fences and this is what they said...
"Hey guys," said Daisy, "How are you doing?"
"Fine thank you," said Rosa the Pug.
"Did you know that my owners are talking about this Coronavirus?" said Bruno the Labrador.
"My owners have been talking a lot about it," said Rosa.
"I love the Coronavirus," said Bruno.
"I do as well!" exclaimed Daisy. "It's great! My owners are always at home so that's really nice and I get lots of walks and attention and cuddles. But I don't really know what Coronavirus is."
"Me neither," said Rosa, "but it's awesome!"

Charlotte Collins (7)

Lockdown

A situation like nothing before ,
has taken the world by surprise and it's nothing we can ignore.
We have to come together to save the ones in need,
come together and succeed.

It may be hard to change our ways,
but we will be the heroes who will deserve the praise.
We may have to live with less freedom and socially distance,
but we must follow rules like these to make a difference.
This situation helps us to appreciate the little things,
like social time, our loved ones and the happiness daily life brings.
So during these times we must keep as busy as possible,
by doing exercise and chatting online, to make these times passable.
We may feel down due to being inside,
or feel anxious about these unknown times,
but we are all in the same boat and have to help each other fight,
so keep your head up and unite!

Maisie Rosetta Moseley (13)

Unity

Unity is when we look after one and another,
Unity is when we care for each other.
No matter what your colour or race,
We don't judge you for your body nor face.

As a community, we unite,
Together we stand, together we fight.
Why be divided, when we can be one?
We're greater than anything, greater than none.

Who says we have to be filled with anxiety,
We care for each other, we are a society!
Free from all possible negativity,
And let's welcome, an old friend, positivity.

Share the love, give the hope, spread the peace,
Let's not be broken, because we can be one piece.
Being judged is a nightmare not a dream,
That's why we are one, we are a team.

So hi, my name is Karina; this is my story,
About unity, peace, and how us, humans, will reach glory!

Karina Palkowska (11)

Stay Strong

C ountless doctors fighting to save lives
O ur community can work together to survive
R acing to aid the sick and poorly
O vertime we will get through this, surely
N ever stop believing and we will succeed
A nd then from this tragedy we will be freed
V aliantly, our nation is working every day
I t has drowned us in sadness but there still is a way
R egular families turned upside-down
U nder this thundercloud affecting every town
S o don't be afraid, just hope this virus will eventually fade.

Haaris Mirzaii (10)

Write To Unite - Together We Stand

Corona Loner

I'm sat here in my bed,
Lying with four pillows under my head
Like all the public forced into quarantine
Videos games all day don't make me too keen!

All the kids who are off school
Think this virus we have is 'so cool'
All the adults who work from their house
Say "Quiet!" while on the phone. "Be just like a mouse!"

Although COVID has messed up my plans
Now all the parks have signs and bans...
Every day from the house is like jail
That's for sure... days go by at the speed of a snail...

Overall when all seems like hell
If you think about it.. it can be swell
Play cards, talk to mates and you'll find
Your boredom will suddenly be left behind!
Don't let the virus get you down...
And turn that frown... upside down!

Jamie Jackson (15)

It's Not All Bad!

Staying at home,
We're all gonna moan.
We're not going to school,
Now that's really not cool.
Hearing people are ill now I'm really scared,
It's all happening so fast I'm really not prepared.
I can't see my friends,
When is this gonna end?
Being stuck indoors,
Now I'm really bored.

But wait it's not all bad,
I don't have to be sad.
When I go for walks, in the windows, what is there?
Inside the windows are rainbows and bears.
Yes I'm stuck at home but my family are here,
So now, I say I have nothing to fear.
Thanks NHS what would we do without you?
You're helping people and also healing them too.
Stand at your doors every Thursday at eight
'Cause we'll clap the NHS yes they really are great!

Isla Stewart (9)

Togetherness

In a time of fear and uncertainty, where the world has capsized, heads full of perplexity and countries on lockdown. Yes, I know this is a time where anxiety rises but let's remember that it's not the end of our lives.

The news is constantly updating us on COVID-19; there's no escaping it but with a nation as determined as us we can get through this. As Her Majesty The Queen said, "If we remain united and resolute, we will overcome it," and it's true.

The NHS staff are doing their best to help tackle the virus and God will help us restore the nation once again. He will fight for us. I just want to let you know that we are in this together. Even though this is scary it's demonstrated that we can work together as one nation.

As Her Majesty The Queen said, "There are better days ahead."

Andel Asare (11)

Let Us Stick Together

The world, as we know, was beautiful and was found with peace, but is now upside down, and a new wreck has risen. You may feel blue, sad on the inside, and totally bored. That virus, the Corona, infected the whole wide world. It's terrifying, isn't it? This is not the end. We will reunite, let every piece of courage and intelligence in our mind work on one thing; teamwork. Nothing can stand in our way. The safety of the whole world is depending on us, and all we are giving is fear and illusions. Well, it'll be no more! Children out there are scared, and parents sacrifice every bit of their blood and mind to calm down their scared kids. Let us team up, fix those scared faces and try to defeat the monstrous Corona. Please stay safe, people's lives depend on your commitment. And remember, don't ever give up!

Abdulelah Mahmoud Alsabhi (10)

Kaleidoscope

A kaleidoscope of emotions
The damaging fog that rolls in devouring my brain
A deep-rooted feeling of lost permeating my veins
In the shadows of doom
I'm powerless
My hands are bound
I am forced to watch
As an unknown force consumes everything I know
The flicker of hope is diming
Longing is but the cruellest of torture
There's a longing to be found
To be united
To be whole
A dark chaos rages through a world that never sleeps
Leaders abandon material feats
For survival needs
A need to work together
Where undervalued are heroes
Slowing the clock to save lives
Together is better even apart
We're hugs are weapons and people are forced to don masks
Let us not forget hope
A kaleidoscope of emotions.

Kimberly Alexis Singer (18)

Stop And Think

When
something
comes into
the world
as fast
as you can blink.
When something comes into the world that makes you stop
and
think. How precious are our
bodies, our family and our
friends. How precious
are the people that
fight for this
to end.
So to everybody   that is feeling
ill today. Let us all just
take a   moment
to send   our love
and   pray.

Albi Perrott Morter (9)

The Bright Side

Look, we are all sad and pitiful but look at the bright side of COVID-19. I have four things to tell you to make your life better but don't expect it to read like a letter.

Hygiene, the definition of that means to be clean. Now look at us washing our hands twenty seconds a day, so all the germs go away.

We get to spend time with family, and we get to play together and jump up and down in our house which is very lovely.

We are helping the environment by not using cars because if we keep destroying the earth, Elon Musk said we have to go to Mars.

We have no silly scammers knocking on our door 24/7, so we can relax and also not pay as much VAT and fuel tax.

So look there is nothing to be sad of and not much that is bad, so look at the bright side and you can be pleasant and glad.

Danyal Rashid (9)

Hope For All

Although these are troubling times,
We must get through, dirt and grime
Through thick and thin we must stand
Altogether hand in hand
We mustn't let ourselves fall
We must have hope for all

Poor Boris was a shock
For that reason we must lock
We must stay in isolation
No matter the frustration
We mustn't let ourselves fall
We must have hope for all

Citizens with their last breaths
NHS with their deaths
Yet forever they will live
With all that they give
We mustn't let ourselves fall
We must have hope for all

Altogether as a nation
We must help this generation
For after the storm
We will all feel warm
We mustn't let ourselves fall
We must have hope for all.

Chloe Dojli (11)

Something To Live For

In everybody's lives, they have a choice;
To live with or without something or someone.
This choice you would think is easy;
But for some it isn't.

We should respect that;
Every person in this world should be treated the same;
No matter how big or small their problem is.
We must listen.

But people's spite and arrogance can take over them;
Creating controversy over different opinions.
We don't want a world like that, do we!
Well we can do a little something to help with that,

In anyone's life, they should have at least a bit of;
Kindness, care, love, peace, faith and hope.
By giving someone these, we can make more of a difference;
Otherwise what is there to live for...

Hanalee Davies (11)

Oh Coronavirus

Oh Coronavirus you're so bad.
Oh Coronavirus you make the people sad.
But on the other hand you make us see
What this planet is turning out to be
We realise we should have seen
How to make our planet clean
But that is no excuse for people dying
And their families crying
Oh Coronavirus you're so bad
Oh Coronavirus you make the people sad
All the countries are staying home
Oh! That's including my home
Oh Coronavirus you're so bad
Oh Coronavirus you make the people sad
We won't stop until you go
And that's why we are going to show
That we will fight together
And that will stay forever
Oh Coronavirus you're so bad
Oh Coronavirus you make the people mad.

Sukhmani Kaur Sidhu (9)

The Best Hope

Who knows how long the storm will last?
Its rattling resonance conquers the sky,
But now, it's a faint memory of the past,
Even the best of storms bid goodbye.

Who knows how long the battle will endure?
As our valiant heroes fight on,
But that ended when peace was adjured,
Even the best of battles are, one day, gone.

As you can see, the sky is shining,
Its wonderful blue woven with white,
Each little white has a silver lining,
Because the best of skies are filled with light.

The hardships of today will be confronted,
Our desire for victory is growing stronger,
Even the best of bad can be bested,
When we courageously join hands with honour.

Aafreen Zainab Kashif (15)

Panic Attacks

And that is when it happened, I can vividly remember the moment. I never felt so trapped inside me, my body was frozen with anger, fear, disgust. But I could show no emotion, all I could do is feel the stream of tears running down my face. Cold. My body was cold, I could now move but I felt like it was too late to do anything. So I just sat there hoping that I would forget about everything that just happened.

I wrote this 'story' to raise awareness to all the children, teens and adults that some people are really struggling during this pandemic. Some might worry because they have a health issue or some might worry that they might lose a loved one. All of these emotions can cause panic attacks, and we have to help people.

Alexandra Matei (14)

The Boy With Odd Powers

This is a strange story about a nine-year-old boy. He was no ordinary kid, he was talented. This child was called Kai, he had the power of dance. I know what you are thinking, boring, but his dancing was special. Let us say he did the moonwalk; he could send anything to the moon. So, if I were you, I would not want to mess with him.

Kai was famous not because of his powers or good looks he was the best skateboarder on earth. At home, he would send dance videos on YouTube and special ones with friends and family. Right now, his focus was to support the NHS and community actively whilst in quarantine.

Keep safe, keep healthy, keep happy entertain yourself however you can.

Bentley Oyenjij (9)

Tulisa's Story

One day the world came to a stop. No school, no playing with friends or going to see our family members and that made me very sad and upset and lonely, but then my head was so so bored I thought I needed to keep busy by going to play on my trampoline. Then I went to watch TV. Then I thought to myself how scary and dangerous this can be, so by staying in it's keeping us all safe. So it's time to make the most of the time with my family at home by sharing happy moments with love and care and helping them through this sort of time, even though we don't know when this will be all over. The day this is all over with I'm going to tell my mum I would like to go and see my friends and family I've missed so much.

Tulisa Louise Steady (7)

Write To Unite - Together We Stand

One Life

Life is a journey we all share
We all go through it fair and square
How we live it, it's up to us
With a negative or with a plus

Life is something to enjoy every day
So take your time to go out and play
Enjoy the time when all goes well
And even when it's bad do not dwell

Enjoy every heartbeat your life is willing to give
Make it count for as long as you live
Follow your passion and you'll do great
Forget about all the things you hate

At the end of the day life is an award
To cherish and keep till you move forward
Love every smile every laughter of fun
Enjoy your life, you only get one.

Janya Balian (13)

Teacup Puppies

T oday, I will get a teacup puppy
E veryone will be so jealous
A s they are cute and expensive
C up puppies are so affectionate
U mm... What are we waiting for? Let's go!
P et store here we come!

P arty time, we're here! Which one shall I get?
U p and down, up and down, the dogs are excited. Hold on, my dream breed
P oodle teacup puppy. Wait! It's sad. I need to cheer it up!
P oor dogs, all unloved, I wish I could take them all!
I am content anyway. I have a pet. I'll call it
E llie! And guess what? She's not
S ad anymore.

Safaa Mahnoor Hosany (10)

Stuck At Home

Now the authorities have declared that the school gates are to shut,
We will need to remain inside our abode even if it's in a hut.
Children like me are now feeling very sad,
We can't go out to play because the pandemic is so bad.
The weather is nice and out comes the sun,
It's unusual that PE now has to be done without a class run.
We need to stay home to protect our community,
Thanks to technology we can contact our friends and keep our unity.
Every day we are making history,
COVID-19 is affecting every country.
Children are learning new skills by studying on Google Classroom,
Our daily commute is now from the lounge back to the bedroom.

Mahveen Ana Chowdhury (8)

COVID-19

Corona, Corona is so deadly,
We can beat this no matter how long it takes,
Our only saviour is the NHS being on the frontline,
We will help them by washing our hands and keeping two metres apart,
Help saves lives by staying in and stopping the spread and please be safe,
Stay in and thank all of our keys workers,
Wash your hands for twenty seconds with soap and hot water,
Don't go out panic buying as there's no need,
If you don't feel well and have any symptoms then please stay at home and ring 111 for help and advice,
Don't meet up with family members or friends outside your house
Please keep everyone safe.

Kayden Holmes (9)

To Our Impeccable NHS And Carers

Oh, whom you care for the sick day and night
Oh, whom every action comes from your heart
Oh, whom with patients you carry the sadness; the pain: of loss and part
Oh, whom Britain could never replace
Oh, whom you are working day and night
Not for money
Not for fame
Not for pleasure
But for lives
But for love
But for strong bonds
Overall, for humanity
And that is why we salute you
Most of all we thank you
It's harder for you than it is for us
Once again, we thank you
Because you are our amazing NHS and our unstoppable carers
With you, we will beat this virus together!

Rola Al-Hassani (11)

Life In Lockdown

Coronavirus – stay inside,
Coronavirus – time to hide,

Entertainment is now history,
A cure for corona what a mystery,
Everything is out of bounds,
Even National Trust have closed their grounds,

Panic buying is all the rage,
Shops are bare - it's all quite strange,

No more pasta,
No more rice,
Things are going up in price,

No more loo roll in the shop,
Coronavirus needs to stop,

No more walks in threes or fours,
Corona's here, lock your doors,

Coronavirus – stay inside,
Coronavirus – time to hide.

Katie Alexandra Cleghorn (14)

2020 Lockdown

Every Thursday night we hang out of our windows and clap,
For the NHS workers all over the world map.
Stay at home, protect the NHS, save lives,
Because the risk of catching this virus is high.
The kids draw rainbows and put them in their windows,
To cheer people up even though at this time, life isn't simple.
Stay two metres apart while out your household,
Or you'll see police around your street wearing uniform in bold.
Only go out once a day for exercise,
Make sure you listen to these rules and be wise.
Stay strong and carry on,
Because one day soon, this crisis will be gone.

Phoebe Grace Ellis (9)

Stay At Home

Due to the trouble we have today,
I have a few words I'd like to say,
I know days are boring and long,
But we need to stay strong,
This has only begun,
But nothing can stop us from having fun,
Why go outside and have a good play,
When you can stay at home and do things all day,
If you're bored try play some games,
You can even try draw red and orange flames,
You might want to read a book,
Maybe one about Captain Hook,
Don't leave your house,
Maybe you can go and catch a mouse,
You know what to do,
If you don't want anything to happen to you.

Lily Razok (10)

Stay Safe! Be Happy!

The world in great danger
Because of the virus there is
To us this virus is a stranger
So it's hard to find a cure

But the NHS do all they can
To help the world with this mess
This has been a serious problem
Since the Easter holidays began

We have no need to worry
Let's just carry on our day
We'll tell this virus to hurry
So we can live the same way

Now thanks to all the people out there who look after each and every one of us
I know we will get through this soon no need to fuss
I wish you all the best of luck.

Ellie Doll Ellis (10)

The Space Tour

It was a fine day when...
In a flash, an alien appeared!
It wasn't a bad alien but it wasn't a good alien either!
I explored space which was insane!
I miss school because of Coronavirus
Although, wow what fun I have had all this time!
When school opens I can tell all my journey!
In the end having amazing and extraordinary fun like a rocket zooming by!

Areej Abdul (9)

Hope It Is

Today will be past, when we find a way at last
Days may be boring but let's keep on going
No work, no school, no fun, no play
But it's not always like this to stay
Days will be bright when we catch a flight, to meet our loved ones around tight
Let's stop being blue and throw away the flu
Keep the spirits high for there's no time to sigh
Together we are, together we will make up for what we have missed
We will rise again, shine again
Roaring and dancing, cheering and laughing
Keeping hope alive for sure we will thrive!

Kairav Ahuja (11)

Fun To Stay At Home

At this point where we all need to stay at home and keep safe.
Many people find it boring and wish to come outside.
Well I can tell you that being at home could be fun and safe!
You can read many stories and imagine you're there,
Draw many beautiful pictures using your imagination where you would like to be.
Spending more time with your family,
And you can also play schools with a family member
Because we still have lots of school work to be done
So while playing schools we can get the real work done too.
Be safe,
Be happy.

Perla Alegra Petkeviciute (9)

Warrior

The days may roll by
Like clouds in a solemn sky
But, amongst the stubborn
Grey of our times
Never forget, that each day we suffer
Is another day closer
To the emergence of the sun
And the rays of liberation it will shine.

And those warriors donned
In apocalyptic uniform
Handling, in perilous proximity
Those whom others are ordered
To distance from in haste:
Will be praised evermore
For their undying sacrifice
To humanity.

Though the bloodshed is great
The promised lands await.

Anik Mitra (16)

Wash Your Hands!

Wash your hands
To fight off infection,
But not to get into
The intesive care section!

Boris Johnson wasn't aware of the problem,
So he ended up in hospital!
This was important so he was heard about
On every single news channel!

COVID-19 is a dangerous virus,
(If you ask me, a really bad disease.)
It's spreading really fast,
Moving from person to person with ease.

We don't know how it started,
But please help out.
Wash your hands every day,
And don't eat sprouts!

Ann Rabea (11)

Coronavirus

- **C** halets are now closed
- **O** utbreaks come only if people spread germs around the place
- **R** arely Africa has germs
- **O** nly go out for a valid reason
- **N** ever put your hands on the face only if your hands are clean
- **A** lways sneeze into your elbows
- **V** anishes only if people stop spreading germs
- **I** nside and outside keep away from people's germs
- **R** egularly wash your hands between 20-40 seconds
- **U** nexpected circumstances in the US
- **S** eriously take good care of yourself.

Hassan Babar

Unite The World

There was a girl called Amy, her only dream was to unite the world. She had a group of friends who tried to say it would be impossible, but she said she would never give up.
When she went home she waited until night then turned into a superhero, uniting girl. She had superpowers to make people like the people who they did not like. Her friends did not know. She had a worst enemy, Ace the Unfriending. He made everyone hate each other. She found Ace and a friend and made them be friends. She made everyone united. She united the world and celebrated with a big party.

Grace Marie Southee (11)

A Message To Coronavirus

- **C** oronavirus go away.
- **O** ur collaboration is stronger than you.
- **R** eally, you made us mad.
- **O** ur lives stopped because of you.
- **N** o one was immune.
- **A** ll of us were affected.
- **V** accines and treatments will be available tomorrow.
- **I** am sure that we will pass this hard time together.
- **R** eturning back to our normal lives will occur tomorrow.
- **U** nited, All of us are going to defeat you.
- **S** taying home was hard but gave families special memories to remember forever.

Hala Mahmoud Radwan (9)

Hospital

On the 24th May 2019, my little sister was born. I was the first person to pick an outfit for her. But my mum's pregnancy was different, she had to test her sugars every day and my little sister was born two weeks earlier than normal babies because my mum had a C-section. The nurses were really kind because they helped my mum with things: testing Reese's (my baby sister) sugars, giving my mum medicine and making sure she could move and walk. So I just wanted to say thank you to all the nurses and midwives who helped my mum through her pregnancy.

Hayden Clutton (10)

Family Fun In Lockdown

Even though we are in lockdown,
We don't have to feel broken down,
Because there is plenty more to do,
When I can't go out with you.

From craft to work,
Homeschooling to plastic making,
We all support a group of people,
The NHS superheroes!

From planning and paying,
To staying and playing,
All of these changes are making an impact on the world.

So stay in,
Stay safe,
And have an excellent time,
Even though we can't meet each other all of the time.

Melissa Lynch (11)

Unite The World

There once was a lady called Iris
She got the blame of the virus
COVID-19 but it can't be seen
We are told it's really mean
Lockdown will not be reviewed on Monday
Every day feels like a Sunday
We miss all our family and all our friends
Let's just hope that this ends
When this is all over I can't wait to see my Gran and Nan,
NHS you're the best, we clap, bang pots and pans
We are your biggest fans
When this is all done we can all have fun
Coronavirus you are done!

Chloe Godfrey

Stay Positive!

Stay positive
Why be blue when you can be yellow?
Don't be a person who is down with a frown
Be a person with a smile
We will beat Coronavirus
We just have to
Stay positive!
Don't be the moon when you can be the sun
Don't be thunder when you can be a rainbow
Don't be a cloud when you
Can be a star
Don't be snow when you
Can be the sunshine
Don't be a tree when you
Can be a flower
Don't be down when you
Can be happy
Stay positive!

Cheyenne Jaycee Mary Walsh (11)

Bored

I am a bit bored you know... My whole diet changed after people were fighting over food. I used to have cake for dessert every day but now all I eat is grass because it is free and people don't fight over it. (That's a joke). Wait a minute I remember people were even fighting over toilet roll. What happened to the saying 'sharing is caring'? But anyway our taxes are stopping because my parents don't go to work. Yay I get to annoy them twice as much. I think I said a bit too much anyway. Goodbye. Remember, stay at home.

Hazel Gonsalves (10)

After The Days Of Quarantine

After the days of quarantine, we will start again
After the days of quarantine, the world will be all new
After the days of quarantine, we will, laugh at this and then
After the days of quarantine, we will be askew.
After the days of quarantine, this all won't sound true.

After the days of quarantine, we can go outside
After the days of quarantine, we won't have to hide
After the days of quarantine, we can all have fun
After the days of quarantine, Brexit we will back as number one.

Alex Pollard

Things I Could Do

It was a really sunny day -
A perfect day to play,
And jump and laugh and have fun
Under the early summer sun,
How I wished to fly to space,
Or go to an exotic place,
And eat ice cream,
Or visit France,
Maybe got to Spain
And learn to dance,
I would dance the tango,
While eating a mango,
Fresh from a farm in Thailand,
With some spring water from the Highlands,
There are so many things to do,
Places to roam,
But right now do your bit,
And stay at home!

Anushree Nikhil Kaluskar (12)

COVID-19

Yet another day of lockdown, I wonder how long it will last. The streets are quiet and the roads are empty. Life is boring, but this time will pass. I'm being positive and this will all end, and life will be back on the mend. But at the moment all we can do is hope for the best. It's a hard test for every country and the governments are trying to make the virus end. We will be able to go out really soon and everybody will be over the moon. But for now we need to follow the Prime Minister's rules so let's all be cool.

Abeera Aftab (11)

Locked In

I mpermissible from leaving
N owhere to go
D igesting all the apathy
O utdoors is definitely a no
O ur surroundings are never changing
R epelling ourselves from leaving
S lowly we are losing it

A ge is steadily creeping
L oathing our houses
W anting to break free
A pplying our new skills
Y outh isn't for eternity
S tay inside, stay protected, save the NHS and save the people infected.

Nehimiah Wairia (13)

Don't Be Scared!

D o as you're told
O r you could get ill
N o matter if your young or old
T ry to keep your distance at the till

B e very positive it will end
E veryone will receive the love we send

S tay at home and you'll be fine
C aring for your family and friends
A ll of us should be kind
R esilience never ends
E veryone will start to shine
D on't be scared and you will find new friends.

Mia Brownbill

Over The Rainbow

One day I woke up and things were a little different, we had to wash our hands at school lots of times, we had to be careful in shops and around family.
Then things started shutting, they closed schools down and parks. There are lots of people dying in the world and it's scary for all of us especially young children like me. Everyone is been super brave and staying safe though so once this sad time ends I'm sure there will be brightness, kindness, love, laughter and a whole new future just over the rainbow.

Annabelle Rose Brett (7)

Never Give Up!

Dear whoever receives this letter,

I understand that in this time of crisis you may feel like a drop in the ocean but all you need to remember is that you are not a drop in the ocean, you are the ocean in a drop. Every time we are going through a rough patch it will make us all stronger but only if you make it. We will all get through this but only if we work together. We all have a role to play whether it is making national decisions or self-isolating, and if we all stick together we can make it through anything!

Lilian Hardill (12)

The Pathway To Triumph!

For the nation, we have loved for years,
Our faith and effort shall polish away the tears,
Thy actions must roar wiseness and care,
Avoiding the faces of sorrow and despair,
Only as one will we overcome this disaster,
By being resolute we can prevent the spread faster,
Let us praise the NHS staff at toil,
Valient and loving, holding our nation up like soil,
So, let us conquer this misfortune together,
By being wise and cooperative, we will continue to endeavour!

Surya Senthilkumar (12)

Wash Your Hands

W ashing your hands is fun
A ll of it is worth it
S oap gets rid of germs
H ope is renewed

Y ou will not get sick if you wash your hands
O h, everyone is healthy
U p in the sky there's no COVID-19
R oll up your sleeves before washing your hands

H ealthiness is here
A ll reunite
N o type of virus will get in our way
D o a great job
S o wash your hands.

Mobolajoko Abigael Olanibijuwon (8)

All In This Together...

In this time of worry and doubt,
We must remember to work as a team,
Being there for each other at all times.

To get through this together,
Appreciate friends and family,
Looking after each other,
Helping and supporting neighbours,
We're all in this together!

Be thankful for our helpful,
Wonderful NHS.
We all love each other,
Looking forward to being together again.
We're all in this together...

We will beat it!

Ellie Attwood (9)

Faith And Hope

I look outside but there is no one there but I have my hope that some day soon, you'll all be there. You will all be standing back by the trees and the grass that blow and just for now, have fun at home. My family is happy and so should you be too, don't let your hopes go because I am still there with you, please know. Thank you NHS and everyone on the frontline. If we all stand together, look after each other we will all be fine.
Love Ruby-Mae, soon we will all be back together one sweet day.

Ruby-Mae Saunders (9)

COVID-19 We Will Survive

COVID-19 we will survive.
Nurses and doctors will help it pass by.
Rainbows in windows
And everyone inside,
If we stay at home we will survive.

COVID-19 we will survive.
We are the United Kingdom
And will stay strong.
A game of hide-and-seek
Will keep us entertained,
Then back to FaceTiming family
Again and again.

COVID-19 we will survive.
Stay at home, protect the NHS, save lives.
Everyone is in this together!

Amelia Fathulla (9)

My Family

My family goes out for fun,
My family strives for the best.
We dance in the rain and sun,
We break through our quests

My family share one blood,
And bloom from just a flower bud.
We hate to give up,
But love to learn and grow.

But sometimes life isn't fair,
And that no one's aware.
We take our challenges,
And hope for the best,
Knowing hope will never fail us,

And keeping us going forever.

Sharanya Sonthalia (11)

Through Death Comes Life

I look out and I see deserted streets, trees calmly swaying in the wind.

I can hear the sound of thriving wild life. Everything is calm, animals are coming out of hiding, the skies are clearer, the smell of smoke and the sound of working factories are gone. This isn't so bad, people all around the world trying to keep morale up. The Coronavirus has given us a chance to reflect on our lives.

This pandemic has taught me one thing: through death comes life.

Dominic O'Brien (11)

Lockdown Boredom

Monday, Tuesday, Wednesday,
They all roll into one.
An endless day of boredom,
That's what the week's become.

On Thursday I did my homework,
Oh no, that isn't true,
Was it Monday, Tuesday, Wednesday?
I haven't got a clue.

Pony Club is cancelled,
Trampolining too.
Rugby isn't happening,
I have nothing left to do.

I didn't want to go to rugby,
Or gymnastics or to school,
But now they are not happening,
I'm bored and it's not cool!

Tess Jacobs (11)

It's Okay

People are crying
And citizens are dying
Hospitals are full
But more are ill
Countries on lockdown
Streets are empty
This is chaos for many

During this global emergency
We should all remain happy
It won't be long
Until this pandemic is gone
Just hold on
It's okay.

Don't worry, don't fret
It hasn't got to you yet
You'll be just fine
It's okay.

Grace Olaoye (11)

A Sight To Behold

Rainbows are elegant,
A sight to behold,
They glimmer in the sky to show a sign of hope,
It's the light in the darkness for those who are sick.

Rainbows are stunning,
A sight to behold,
Wiping away the pain for those young and old,
And giving a blanket to those who are cold.

Rainbows are pretty,
A sight to behold,
Taking the worry from those who heed,
Putting a smile on those who are weak.

David Baffour Atuahene Ofosuhene (12)

Lockdown

L ost opportunities - no trips to the park.
O ur lives are on pause; my mood is quite dark.
C an we survive this? Sometimes I worry.
K eep feeling bored as there's no need to hurry.
D ays are relaxed. I start to unwind.
O ur thoughts turn to others; we have time to be kind
W hat have I gained? Time for family; time for me.
N ow it feels normal. What's next? We'll see.

Emily Rose Pettitt (12)

My Teachers

T he world would never become without our teachers
E veryone finds their place in the world with them
A nd give us experiences like no other
C alling out to all teachers in the world
H ere at home, it is more lonely than ever
E veryone pulling sad faces, more than ever
R eunite everyone and we can pull this off together
S lowly it will go, but we need more help than ever before!

Daljit Singh Virk (11)

Acrostic Poem On Lockdown

L ots of baking to do at home and other activities inside the house
O nly go out for essentials
C an't go to school, cinemas, restaurants or parks
K eeping indoors to save lives
D on't forget to wash your hands thoroughly
O nly key workers go to work to help us all
W e wish everything settles down and goes back to normal
N urses look after patients and are very brave.

Simra Noor Aziz (8)

Key Job Mania

Once there was a key worker called Danny. Yep he is a rabbit! He works at a hospital day and night. The hospital was in west Lothian. He was saving lives during the COVID-19 lockdown. He travels by train.
He woke up from his twelve-hour sleep and knew that he was late so he rushed like a fox would do to steal and run away! Ten minutes later he was at the hospital and he wore a mask, a baby-sized mask. He saved a bunch of lives and defeated the virus.

Kesley Brito

Staying Home

S taying home for each twenty-four-hour period,
T V to charm me on,
A very long game of Minecraft mini-games,
Y ippee! I finally won,

A yummy jam toast with a giant hot chocolate mug,
T imetable saying is time to work

H appy chatting with the family,
O h it only has just begun,
M y job is easy to do,
E ven you should do this too!

Ryan Ashton Ashton Moyo (10)

Doctors Acrostic

- **D** o not go out of your home during this pandemic.
- **O** nly go out to buy food, medicine or work if you a keyworker.
- **C** are for the vulnerable elderly people when you stay at home.
- **T** ogether we can beat this deadly virus.
- **O** nly if you obey the rule to stay at home.
- **R** ead books and be creative while on lockdown.
- **S** tay safe at home to protect yourself, others and our amazing NHS.

Michael Akintayo Akinwonmi-Pedro (9)

Animals Of The World

Animals too are created with love,
By our God who lives above.
He made them in different forms,
By land, by sea and by air they are born.

Some animals can be kept,
To live with us as a pet.
Other animals want to live free,
Just like a wild bee.

When God created the animals in the sea,
He was filled with glee.
The whales, the fish are free,
To swim around with others to see.

Alexander Pagtalunan Church (11)

Key Worker

I often think about what I would like to be,
Then I put on the TV and I see,
It's someone that will look after me,
I often think could I really amount to someone so brave,
courageous and stronger,
Then I no that I would belong,
I want to be on the front line like them,
Be someone that is the structure like a flowers stem,
They help them in need,
That's what I would like to be.

Lola Marshall

Positivity

Yes, Coronavirus is really here
and hospitals are really near,
but put that away
and let's hear you say,
that it won't be forever,
never, never, never!

You still have to be two metres away,
even if it's a warm sunny May,
but you can still have fun
in the sun.
Invent a new game perhaps?

Spend time together,
it won't be forever!

Aneta Charvatova (10)

Write To Unite - Together We Stand

Protect Our National Heroes Service

S trong-willed humans fighting against villains.
T rying to stop COVID-19.
A n illness many are afraid of.
Y awning in boredom.

A way from light.
T rying to follow the rules,

H ope for the best.
O bserve and take in information daily.
M ake the best whilst at home.
E veryone can fight Corona.

Aemon Blake Adiz (10)

The Story Of Worries Of Coronavirus

Everyone knows about Coronavirus but not to make you worried. People have Coronavirus so don't go near people. If you sneeze then you need to wash your hands and when I say wash your hands I don't mean put on hand sanitiser. For example my mum told me to wash my hands but instead of washing my hands I just put on my hand sanitiser even though there's a sink right next to me. That is just crazy.

Emaan Ali Khan

Thank You

Thank you.
To the NHS, for saving people's lives.
Thank you.
To key workers, providing us with essential services.
Thank you.
To the people who are staying at home, in order to flatten the curve.
Thank you.
To the volunteers, buying food for the vulnerable.
Thank you.
You are helping us get through these worrying times.
We will work together; in unity.

Megan Powell (12)

My Name

K enzie is my name
E vie is my best friend
N o way am I giving up! Some animals do this to survive!
Z ebras galloping
I guanas hiding
E lephants trumpeting

A t home you can learn
V iolin, learn to play
E xercise or email
Y esterday was a fun day, and today is going to be too!

Kenzie Sarah Jane Avey (8)

Stay Safe

Stay at home, because
COVID-19 is in town
Be safe and sound
Make sure your
Friends and family
Don't come round
Extra lives will
Save breaths, because
COVID-19 is in town
Say thanks to the
NHS because they're
Saving lives will help.
Boris Johnson would
be very thankful
Please be safe
Everyone.

Miley Goodman (9)

A Promise

We are just in our homes,
Frozen like sticks and stones.
We can't go out,
And the people still doubt;
About our lives
And that we will survive.
The virus doesn't take pity!
But when this goes our way,
We will go to school like a normal day.
And we can only pray to God almighty.
This will soon pass and go away!

Rylan Miguel Longog Medina-Longog (9)

We Can Fight COVID-19 Together

After a stormy day there is always a bright, shiny rainbow. And that shows we can fight this together, don't worry! If you keep a nice smiling face you shall be okay. I am here for you, so don't give up! If you survive this than you shall become part of the rainbow, keep up with your dreams we will all be okay and get through this together I promise.

Savannah Rose H (10)

Thank You NHS

Lost loved ones
Cause seas of tears
But we need to stay strong
And fight our fears

We will stay strong
And never give in
So cough into a tissue
And put it in the bin

So I thank very dearly
The ones who fight for lives
The ones who work so very hard
To try and help us survive.

Muzn Hassan (10)

Happiness

H aving fun
A nd restoring hope
P eople working together
P ersevering to keep safe
I n dangerous times staying strong
N ever giving up
E ven when there are hard times
S unlight helping us to see in the day
S ometimes you have to believe in the world.

Ruby Jones (9)

Stay At Home!

S unshine and hot weather,
T V? Nah, camp in the garden,
A nd eat yummy ice cream
Y es!

A nd spooky stories
T en-thousand stars will join us together.

H ide-and-seek?
O f course.
M ore ice cream?
E veryone dance and sing.

Jagoda Kramarz (9)

My Acrostic Poem For Doctors

- **D** octors keep us healthy and safe and help us when we're ill
- **O** n the call to save our lives
- **C** arrying patients to the wards
- **T** o give them the medicine they need
- **O** h we really have to thank them
- **R** unning around to bring patients in
- **S** o thank you, helpful doctors!

Priya Bose (9)

It's Okay

My mummy says it's okay not to be okay.
To feel like you'll go crazy if you stay home another day.
To miss your friends and going out to play.
Because by staying home every day.
We will be okay.
Eventually there will come a beautiful day.
When we can all run and skip and play.
We will be okay.

Hollie Smith (9)

Rules

D on't meet others outside your household
O nly go outside for basic provisions
C an you please stay two metres apart?
T ogether we will get through this!
O nly go outside to provide essentials for the vulnerable
R ules that are here to make sure everyone is safe.

Scarlett Anne Pattinson (10)

Attention: Stay Home!

Attention: stay home!
Look up the news on Chrome
Don't joke with your safety
That might get you negativity
Coronavirus is scary
Maybe creepy
But don't you worry
But Coronavirus is not a story
Stay clean
Even if you're a teen
The message is stay safe at home.

Zlata Strelkova (9)

Together As One!

The Coronavirus is a task set
That no one will forget
Every Thursday we give a clap
To show our respect to NHS and wish them good luck.

Boris Johnson has worked hard for us
So we need to show our trust
We also draw a beautiful rainbow
To represent our love through the window.

Houda Mountaser (10)

Rainbows And Sunshine

Rainbows and sunshine
It's not such a fun time
Staying at home
It's got to be done
But it is at least fun
This should be over soon
But just look at the sun at noon
It's shining bright not in fright
So think of rainbows and sunshine to lift your spirits high.

Olivia Poltorak (8)

Rainbow

- **R** ainbows in every window,
- **A** reminder of brighter days.
- **I** f we all stay indoors,
- **N** HS will survive and
- **B** oris will give us his praise.
- **O** ut of the lockdown, in time we will come.
- **W** e did it together, now starts the fun.

Nia Davies (12)

Do I Really Understand It?

C oronavirus puts us in danger
O h no! Some people are dying
V ery bad things are happening
I s there anything we can do about it
D o something about it

1 00% of social distancing required
9 99 are helping

Troie Kannasizam Oranyendu (8)

We Are The Rainbow Children

Rainbows, rainbows drew by us put in the windows
Rainbows, rainbows help us look on the bright side
Rainbows, rainbows for our NHS
Rainbows, rainbows so colourful and bright
Rainbows, rainbows help us carry on
Rainbows, rainbows brighten our days.

Isabelle Palmer (9)

Rainbow Acrostic

- **R** aining outside
- **A** dventure awaits
- **I** nside my house
- **N** ot knowing what to do
- **B** ored of staying in
- **O** ut comes the sun
- **W** ith a rainbow brightening up my day.

Adina Jashari

Coronavirus

Coronavirus you are bad!!
Coronavirus you make people sad.
Coronavirus you are fast to snatch
Coronavirus you are easy to catch.
Coronavirus go away!!
Coronavirus don't come back another day!!

Lenard Williams (8)

Nurse

N urses look out for us when we are sick
U nderstanding they can do a good trick.
R ecommending medicines for us.
S eeing what is wrong.
E verybody is working for our NHS.

DyuthiMohan Tulasi (9)

The View Outside!

When I wake up,
I pull the window up,

I see the sun rise,
As I sigh,

As the flowers bloom,
I wake up from a total gloom,

When I shout hooray,
The flowers rise!

Abeeshana Ariyararatnam (11)

To Key Workers

To key workers, thanks for all of your help key workers, I know that we are living in a disaster right now but I am sure it will end. Dad you are my hero.

Reem Taan (7)

WRITE TO UNITE WAS BROUGHT TO YOU BY YOUNG WRITERS

We hope you have enjoyed reading this book – and that you will continue to in the coming years.

If you're a young writer who enjoys reading and creative writing, or the parent of an enthusiastic poet or story writer, do visit our website **www.youngwriters.co.uk**. Here you will find free competitions, workshops and games, as well as recommended reads, a poetry glossary and our blog. There's lots to keep budding writers motivated to write!

If you would like to order further copies of this book, or any of our other titles, then please give us a call or order via your online account.

Young Writers
Remus House
Coltsfoot Drive
Peterborough
PE2 9BF
(01733) 890066
info@youngwriters.co.uk

We're delighted that £1 from every sale of a Write To Unite book is donated to NHS Charities Together Registered Charity No 1186569

Join in the conversation!
Tips, news, giveaways and much more!

YoungWritersUK   @YoungWritersCW